AF269668

The *Rosary* {.title}

in my pocket

Compiled by
the Daughters of St. Paul

Illustrated by
Mary Joseph Peterson, FSP

Illustrator Assistant
Laura Rosemarie McGowan, FSP

Pauline
BOOKS & MEDIA
Boston

The Rosary

We pray the Rosary to honor Jesus and his Mother Mary. We use a set of beads. We say a prayer as we touch each bead. We think about some important times in the lives of Jesus and Mary as we pray. These important times are called the mysteries of the Rosary. The chart on these two pages will show you how to pray the Rosary, step by step.

4. Pray the Glory
Name the 1st mystery
Pray the Our Father

5. Pray 10 Hail Marys

14. Pray the Glory
and the Hail,
Holy Queen (page 15)

3. Pray 3
Hail Marys

15. Kiss the crucifix

2. Pray the Our Father

1. Make the
Sign of the Cross
and pray the
Apostles' Creed

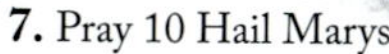

7. Pray 10 Hail Marys

6. Pray the Glory
Name the 2nd mystery
Pray the Our Father

8. Pray the Glory
Name the 3rd mystery
Pray the Our Father

9. Pray 10 Hail Marys

13. Pray 10 Hail Marys

10. Pray the Glory
Name the 4th mystery
Pray the Our Father

12. Pray the Glory
Name the 5th mystery
Pray the Our Father

11. Pray 10 Hail Marys

The Prayers of the Rosary

The Sign of the Cross

In the name of the Father, and of the Son, and of the Holy Spirit. Amen.

Our Father

Our Father, who art in heaven, hallowed be thy name. Thy kingdom come, thy will be done on earth as it is in heaven. Give us this day our daily bread, and forgive us our trespasses, as we forgive those who trespass against us. And lead us not into temptation, but deliver us from evil. Amen.

Hail Mary

Hail Mary, full of grace, the Lord is with you. Blessed are you among women, and blessed is the fruit of your womb, Jesus. Holy Mary, Mother of God, pray for us sinners, now and at the hour of our death. Amen.

Glory

Glory to the Father, and to the Son, and to the Holy Spirit: as it was in the beginning, is now, and will be for ever. Amen.

The Apostles' Creed

I believe in God, the Father almighty,
    creator of heaven and earth.

I believe in Jesus Christ, his only Son, our Lord.
    He was conceived by the power of the Holy
        Spirit
      and born of the Virgin Mary.
    He suffered under Pontius Pilate,
      was crucified, died, and was buried.
    He descended to the dead.
    On the third day he arose again.
    He ascended into heaven,
      and is seated at the right hand of the
        Father.
    He will come again to judge the living and
      the dead.

I believe in the Holy Spirit,
    the holy catholic Church,
    the communion of saints,
    the forgiveness of sins,
    the resurrection of the body,
    and the life everlasting. Amen.

The
Joyful Mysteries

*We pray the joyful mysteries
on Mondays and Saturdays.*

Jesus, the joyful mysteries
remind me of when you were
a baby and a child. As I greet
your Mother, I will think of
how she watched and helped
you to grow in wisdom and
grace.

1. The Annunciation
of the Archangel to Mary

Mary becomes the
Mother of God.

2. The Visitation

Mary visits St. Elizabeth.

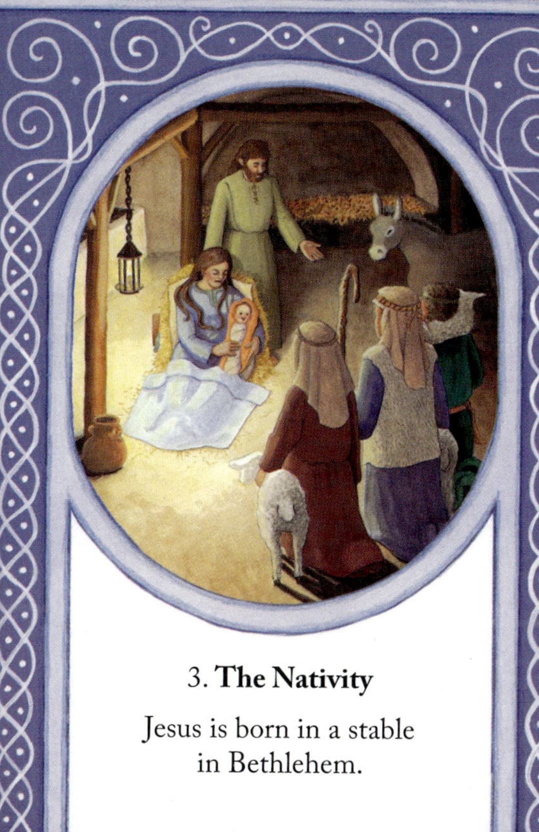

3. **The Nativity**

Jesus is born in a stable
in Bethlehem.

4. The Presentation in the Temple

Mary and Joseph present
Jesus to God.

5. The Finding of Jesus in the Temple

Mary and Joseph find Jesus talking about God his Father.

The Mysteries of Light

We pray the mysteries of light on Thursdays.

Jesus, the mysteries of light remind me about things you did when you were all grown up. As I pray, I will think about how you taught the people about God your Father and the kingdom of heaven. I will ask Mary to keep me close to you.

1. The Baptism of Jesus

John baptizes Jesus.

2. The Wedding at Cana

Jesus works his first miracle.

3. Jesus Announces God's Kingdom

Jesus teaches the people to turn their hearts to God.

4. The Transfiguration

Jesus shines
with the glory of God.

5. Jesus Gives Us the Holy Eucharist

Jesus changes bread and
wine into his Body and Blood.

The Sorrowful Mysteries

We pray the sorrowful mysteries on Tuesdays and Fridays.

Jesus, the sorrowful mysteries remind me of your suffering and death. I will pray, thinking of how much you suffered to save us from sin. I will ask your Mother Mary to help me to accept my own sufferings out of love for you.

1. The Agony in the Garden

Jesus suffers and prays.

2. The Scourging at the Pillar

Jesus is whipped.

3. **The Crowning with Thorns**

The soldiers make fun
of Jesus.

4. The Carrying of the Cross

Jesus carries his heavy cross.

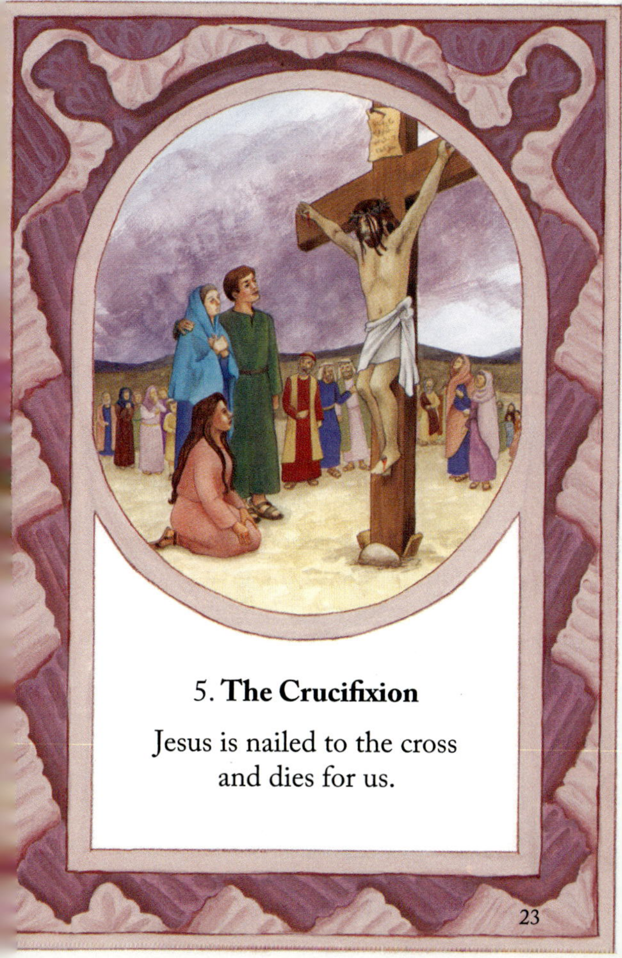

5. **The Crucifixion**

Jesus is nailed to the cross
and dies for us.

The
Glorious Mysteries

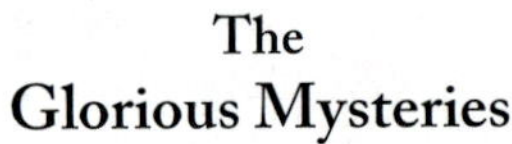

*We pray the glorious mysteries
on Wednesdays and Sundays.*

Jesus, the glorious mysteries make me think of your
victory over death. They also
remind me of the gifts you
gave your most holy Mother.
As I pray, I will remember
that if I stay close to you,
I will be happy with you
forever in heaven some day.

1. The Resurrection

Jesus rises from the dead.

2. The Ascension

Jesus goes back to heaven.

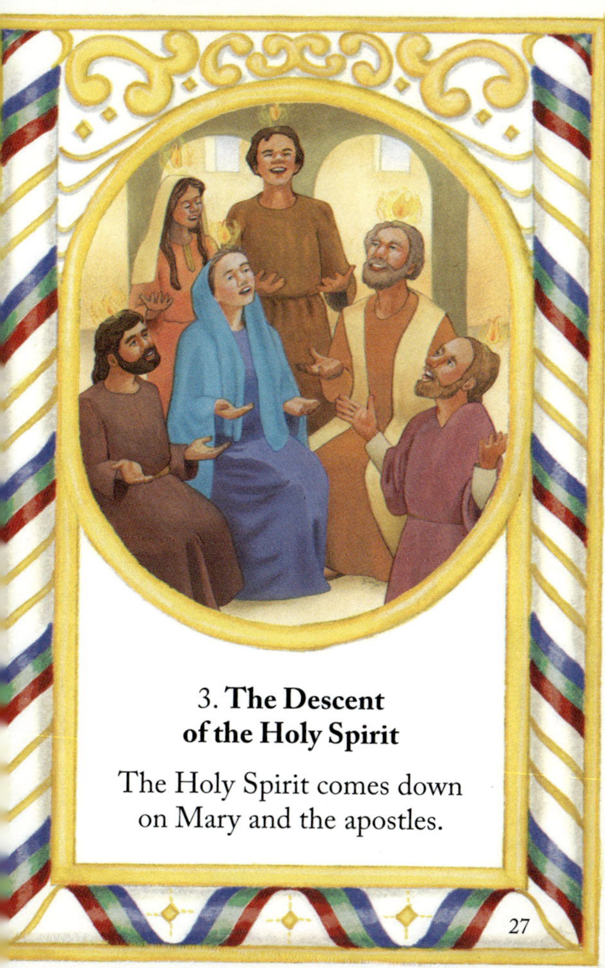

3. **The Descent of the Holy Spirit**

The Holy Spirit comes down on Mary and the apostles.

4. The Assumption

Mary is taken body and soul
to heaven.

5. The Coronation

Mary is crowned
Queen of heaven and earth.

After the Glory at the end of each of the 10 Hail Marys, we may also say the prayer that Mary taught the children when she appeared at Fatima.

The Prayer Mary Taught Us at Fatima

O my Jesus, forgive us our sins, save us from the fires of hell. Lead all souls to heaven, especially those most in need of your mercy.

Hail, Holy Queen

Hail, holy Queen, Mother of mercy, our life, our sweetness, and our hope. To you do we cry, poor banished children of Eve; to you do we send up our sighs, mourning and weeping in this valley of tears. Turn then, most gracious advocate, your eyes of mercy toward us; and after this our exile, show unto us the blessed fruit of your womb, Jesus. O clement, O loving, O sweet Virgin Mary.

Short Prayers to Mary

We come to you for help,
holy Mother of God.
Please hear our prayers.
Save us from anything that could hurt
us, glorious and blessed Virgin.

My dear Mother Mary, keep me safe
in your care. Make my thoughts,
desires, words, and actions holy so that
I may please you and your Jesus, my
God. I want to live with you for ever
in heaven someday. Amen.

I am all yours, and all that I have, I
give to you, dear Jesus, through Mary,
your holy Mother.

CALIFORNIA
3908 Sepulveda Blvd, Culver City, CA 90230   310-397-8676
2640 Broadway Street, Redwood City, CA 94063   650-369-4230
5945 Balboa Avenue, San Diego, CA 92111   858-565-9181

FLORIDA
145 S.W. 107th Avenue, Miami, FL 33174   305-559-6715

HAWAII
1143 Bishop Street, Honolulu, HI 96813   808-521-2731
Neighbor Islands call: 866-521-2731

ILLINOIS
172 North Michigan Avenue, Chicago, IL 60601   312-346-4228

LOUISIANA
4403 Veterans Memorial Blvd, Metairie, LA 70006   504-887-7631

MASSACHUSETTS
885 Providence Hwy, Dedham, MA 02026   781-326-5385

MISSOURI
9804 Watson Road, St. Louis, MO 63126   314-965-3512

NEW JERSEY
561 U.S. Route 1, Wick Plaza, Edison, NJ 08817   732-572-1200

NEW YORK
150 East 52nd Street, New York, NY 10022   212-754-1110

PENNSYLVANIA
9171-A Roosevelt Blvd, Philadelphia, PA 19114   215-676-9494

SOUTH CAROLINA
243 King Street, Charleston, SC 29401   843-577-0175

TENNESSEE
4811 Poplar Avenue, Memphis, TN 38117   901-761-2987

TEXAS
114 Main Plaza, San Antonio, TX 78205   210-224-8101

VIRGINIA
1025 King Street, Alexandria, VA 22314   703-549-3806

CANADA
3022 Dufferin Street, Toronto, ON M6B 3T5   416-781-9131